SOUTHERN REGION FLASHBACK:

the South Western main line through Hampshire in the 1950s

Compiled by David Kimber

ISBN 978-1-906419-66-0

First published in 2011 by Kevin Robertson under the **NOODLE BOOKS** imprint
PO Box 279 Corhampton, SOUTHAMPTON SO32 3ZX

www.noodlebooks.co.uk

Printed in England by The Information Press.

Front cover - BR built No. 35025 'Brocklebank Line', at No. 7 Gates, 500 yards east of Brockenhurst. (JK)

Rear Cover - Brockenhurst Goods Yard. (JK)

Frontispiece - Freight in the Forest, including a salt wagon. No 31632 is climbing Sway Bank deep in the heart of the New Forest heath land. (JK)

Opposite - A youthful David Kimber posed alongside a rather older sign directing the public to the station at Brockenhurst. The year is 1964 and lifting barriers have just been installed at the nearby Lyndhurst Road crossing. (JK)

Introduction

The photographs in this the first half of this book have been selected from the never-published collection of my late father, John Kimber, 1922-2004 (JK). I did not appear on the scene until 1960 so nearly all the images predate me but the locations became very familiar to me as a train-mad youngster growing up in the New Forest.

My father's photographic outings became more frequent as the end of steam on the Southern Region approached, with Sway Bank, just outside Brockenhurst a favourite location. Here Bournemouth and Weymouth -bound services were usually working hard on the 1 in 103 climb and apart from the memorable sight, and sound, of steam there was the additional excitement for a young lad of lineside fires to extinguish. (I recall reading once about how Waterloo were delighted that with the end of steam it would also bring to an end litigation for damage to crops and the lineside.) The extinguishing of the results of such pyrotechnics was frequently used as an excuse by my father when we returned home late (again) for tea, although the delayed appearance of the down 'Royal Wessex' was, in all honesty, the more likely cause. Happy days.

Although reference has been made to father's images from the end of steam, those contained within this book have been deliberately selected to cover a slightly earlier period, with in the later pages, the work of two other contemporary photographers, Henry Meyer (HM) and Edward Griffiths (EG).

David Kimber

Bournemouth 2011

Left - Prior to a revision of the county boundary, Bournemouth was in the county of Hampshire, certainly so at the time the photographs on these pages were taken. To be fair we are taking it to the very edge with the inclusion of part of the Branksome triangle, although I doubt there will be too many complaints with the scene. The 'Bournemouth Belle' is photographed at the start of its journey recorded between the West and Central stations at Bournemouth. The arm of the triangle nearest the camera carries the main line from Bournemouth towards Weymouth and is still in use today. Out of sight was a third viaduct completing the triangle which allowed trains from Bournemouth West to take the west chord towards Poole, it was this arm that was used by services to and from the erstwhile Somerset & Dorset route. (This latter viaduct is still in use today affording access to the EMU maintenance depot.) The Bullied Pacific seen is about to cross over a very quiet Surrey Road. All three viaducts still remain intact although only two retain track. (JK)

Right - Arriving at Bournemouth West, No. 76010 with what may well be empty stock. (JK)

Left - The interloper at Bournemouth West, LMS 2P No. 40697 easily identified as approaching with a train from the Somerset & Dorset line. After arrival and with the stock drawn off, the engine will reverse back to the shed at Branksome to be turned and serviced ready for the return working. (JK)

Right - Probably performing station pilot duties - such as drawing back the stock from the train seen arriving opposite - M7 No. 30112 is almost the centre of attention to the waiting passengers. From the glimpse of the signal on the right, the engine of the departing service carried a little more impact! (JK)

Left - We move eastwards now in contemporary Hampshire proper and to the locomotive depot at Bournemouth Central. Here John Kimber is clearly in the shed area itself although most of the comings and goings could also be viewed from the platform at the west end of the station. There was also the famous notice on the boundary wall 'Quiet Please Residential Area', private accommodation then backing right to the edge of the shed area. How it was possible to keep quiet at a steam shed was perhaps easier said than done. Three SR locomotives are visible, all of the 4-6-0 type, nearest the camera No. 30855, to the right No. 30743 and in the background a second member of the 'King Arthur' class. (JK)

Right - An effortless climb of Sway Bank for the westbound 'Royal Wessex' with its green-painted Mk1 coaching stock, the Lymington branch line visible through the bridge. Westbound trains often struggled up this climb, mostly following a stop at Brockenhurst station. The railway thoughtfully left fire-beaters by the next footbridge 500 yards up the bank, so passers-by (and train photographers) might prevent a small fire spreading to the surrounding heathland. Today the view is completely obscured by foliage. (JK)

Top left - Views of Lymington Junction west of Brockenhurst where not just the branch to the former coastal town diverged, but also the junction with the 'old road' to Ringwood and Wimborne. The up home signal for trains from Lymington can be seen whilst the double junction for the Ringwood Line - also known as the 'Castlemans Corkscrew' is in the foreground. No. 30782 'Sir Brian' has charge of what is an inter-regional working complete with carriage roof boards, although the name cannot be identified. The train carries the standard BR 'A' class headcode for principal passenger services, as compared with the route codes that were common on the Southern Region. (Inter-regional services retained their originating headcode positions when arriving on Southern metals.) The train is heading west towards Bournemouth, the roof of Lymington Junction signal box just visible above the tender of the engine. (JK)

Bottom left - No. 35025 seen for a second time and again on the 'Royal Wessex'. (The fact the same engine appears on different days perhaps indicates that at the time this engine was regarded as a "good-un' at Nine Elms.) The stock is also interesting with a red and cream (carmine and cream is perhaps slightly more accurate) rake of Mk1 vehicles supplemented at the front by a Bulleid vehicle. Whilst having recording locations it is perhaps unfortunate that dates were not always noted. For consistency the decision was taken to exclude dates from the collection rather than risk inaccuracies. (JK)

Right - Taking the old road to the west at Lymington Junction. Some stopping services, even Bulleid Pacific-hauled, were deliberately sent by this route although it also served as valuable diversion with trains able to continue to Weymouth or arrive at Bournemouth via Poole. (JK)

Left - Alone in the New Forest, No. 30531 quietly drifts down Sway Bank whilst the evening sun casts its shadow . The bridge with the fire-beaters referred to earlier is in the background. (JK)

Right - Sister engine No. 30532 arriving at Lymington Junction, the signalman ready to receive the single line tablet from an unseen fireman. At this time there was still a physical junction at this point, the train about to join the Up main line, consequently the signalman has of necessity to lean some way over . Although the train following is out of camera, this was likely to have been a freight as the driver is looking back, possibly to check with the guard. With the battery box on the framing just ahead of the cab, No. 30532 is seen to be AWS-fitted compared with No. 30531 opposite. Today the physical junction is no more, a dedicated line for the branch running parallel with the main line from Brockenhurst station. (JK)

Above - 'Push-Pull' at Lymington Junction, a branch train being propelled on to the branch with the driver about to collect the tablet, this time from the carrier rather than the signalman. In the opposite direction, branch trains were often given the priority over main line workings. This ensured a connection could be made for passengers wishing to continue their journey. (JK) **Right -** If only the sound had been recorded as well, H15 No. 30489 accelerating rapidly past the western end of Brockenhurst down sidings with what is either a stopping or relief Bournemouth service. (JK)

Left - Shunting in Brockenhurst up-side yard. The station is on the right with the footbridge just visible over the roof of the parcels office (complete with long line of fire buckets). The area occupied by the train is now the station car-park although the goods shed has survived - as an Italian restaurant. As children, my friends and I were convinced shunting only ever took place in this yard when we were asleep - the wagons seemed to be a different position very day but we never saw a locomotive - giving rise to the 'midnight shunter' theory. The Morris Traveller parked outside the parcels office was probably my father's, he certainly owned a number of them, presumably the result of living next door to the Morris dealership at Waters Green in Brockenhurst. I remember (only too well) being cooped up in the back on long journeys, particularly the day-long trek to Cornwall for summer holidays. (JK)

Right - Shunting in the up-side sidings. (JK)

No 35016 'Elder Fyffes' getting into its stride leaving Brockenhurst for Bournemouth - with a little help from the steam sanding gear. The bridge in the background at the west end of the station was known locally as the 'Black Bridge' as opposed to the 'White Bridge' at the Southampton end of the station. Curiously the former has now been closed in but on the Bournemouth side only. On the left the siding leads to the goods yard and shed seen previously, with the end wall of the Parcels Office just visible through the bridge. Brockenhurst had four platform faces, left to right Nos. 1 to 4. No. 1 was used as an up relief and also for Ringwood line services, Nos. 2 and 3 for Up and Down main line workings - the train seen is leaving Platform 3 - and Platform 4 as an Up loop and also for the Lymington branch trains. On the right are the carriage sidings. (JK)

No. 30748 passing under Black Bridge and slowing for the Brockenhurst stop. This footbridge was very low and tantalisingly close to passing trains, making it a favourite place to while away the hours in my youth. Laying down and squinting through the (rather large) gaps in the planks was a favourite pastime resulting in a satisfying face full of smoke and cinders from expresses racing through Brockenhurst station. Apart from the lamented steam engine, so much else visible that was so also typically Southern has disappeared over the years. (JK)

BROCKENHURST

Left - Apparently catching Dad by surprise was LMS built diesel-electric No. 10000 as it races through Brockenhurst bound for Southampton Central and Waterloo - he normally placed his trains better than in this shot. I am not sure what the speed limit was through the station at this time, possibly 60 mph, but Up trains had the benefit of the descent from Sway and would often hold on to as much speed as possible ready for the ascent to Woodfidley and Beaulieu Road - this climb commencing soon after passing through the station. Speaking of speed, I remember a summers evening towards the end of steam on the Southern, standing with Dad at the Bournemouth end of Platform 2, when an up express came hurtling towards the station, bucking and rolling alarmingly over the points by the signalbox. Dad was uncharacteristically worried, telling me to dive for cover if the train left the track, which seemed quite likely. It didn't, of course, but his intended photograph was completely missed on that occasion. (JK)

Above - A clean Q1, No. 33002 takes a break from shunting duties. (JK)

Right - A Ringwood line train in Platform 1 - health and safety hazards aplenty on the platform! Just beyond the footbridge was an unusual swingbridge linking the forecourt to Platforms 1 & 2. This was provided when the station was enlarged in 1888, the same time as the direct line through Sway was opened. It was intended as a barrow / trolley route so avoiding the stairs, but was frequently used for passenger access, particularly at peak school hours. A similar swingbridge existed at Eastleigh for many years. (JK)

Left - The London end of the station with an engine changeover taking place with a Lymington - Waterloo working. Through workings to the branch line were common on summer Saturdays, although locomotive restrictions on the Lymington branch meant the main line engine would often need to be changed. Here Lord Nelson No. 30861 'Lord Anson' draws forward before setting back into Platform 1 and its waiting train. This has been brought up the branch by the 'Q' class 0-6-0 No. 30541, the tender of which is just in the frame and is seen more clearly below, No. 30541 having drawn forward and clear to allow the changeover to take place. (Both JK)

Right - No. 34070 'Manston' departing for Southampton and Waterloo. (JK)

Left - Brockenhurst 'A' signal-box and level crossing at the London end of the station. Here the railway dissected the Lyndhurst - Lymington main road, the A337. Having its origins with the LSWR, by this time various seemingly ad-hoc additions had been made resulting in a decidedly ramshackle appearance. It was replaced soon afterwards by a signalbox contemporary on the opposite side of the line to the west side of the road crossing. (JK)

Opposite inset - seen from the rear the various additions are again visible. Immediately behind is one of the gatekeepers cottages provided on the original Southampton and Dorchester railway. Each were identified by a number, this being No. **7.** (JK)

Right - A close up of No. 7 gates, 500 yards east of the A337 road crossing. This was a foot crossing which was superseded by a concrete footbridge in the late 1950s. (JK)

The type of engine as well as the position of the head-code discs clearly indicates this to be a Bournemouth to Brighton through train, former LBSCR Atlantic, No. 32425 'Trevose Head' departing from Platform 2 and getting away. The Atlantics were changed with many of these workings in early BR days subsequently being replaced by a variety of motive power, almost as if none were considered equal to the older design. (JK)

The same engine but this time in the opposite direction approaching Brockenhurst. Despite the age of the engine, built in 1911, it is attached to a modern 4-coach BR Mk1 set, No. 870, some 40 years younger. A loose coach has also been added at the end of the set. On the right is a pristine concrete permanent-way hut, the product of the SR concrete works at Exmouth Junction. These were designed with a sloping roof so as to be 'in-gauge' if transported to site on a rail wagon, and were then lifted off by crane. Other times a kit of parts might arrive to be assembled on site. (JK)

Another veteran, L class No. 31777, this time dating from 1914. The train is also considerably shorter so possibly a relief working. Members of the L class that survived into the 1950s were allocated to various SR sheds including Nine Elms and Brighton. It was very much a question of finding suitable work for them, hence this appearance far from its original haunts in the south-east. (JK)

No. 31621, almost at the end of its journey at Brockenhurst although the train will continue with a different engine the last few miles to Lymington. The view is taken at No. 7 gates and from the replacement footbridge at this location referred to previously. The signals are for the main line through the station and also for the down loop, Platform 4. Speaking to a man who had once lived in the crossing cottage it was natural to ask him how he ever managed to sleep with his bedroom 10' from passing trains. No doubt he had become used to the noise as he replied that generally they helped him get to sleep, although he did recall being woken one night by a freight struggling to stop at the signals, the engine whistling furiously and the brake blocks of many of the wagons glowing red in the night. (JK)

Trains at No. 7 Gates before the provision of the 'White Bridge'. Both the workings seen are Up trains, the variety of locomotives and stock so typical of the period. In the left view two brick chimneys can just be seen above the roof of the third coach. These were part of the 'Motant Arms' PH, now closed but at the time one of three pubs within a quarter of a mile of Brockenhurst station, making it a favourite stopping-off point for the thirsty traveller. .

A personal memory from this location is of the longest, loudest and most piercing whistle I have ever heard. The guilty party was a 'Hall' class engine on the afternoon through working from the Midlands which whistled incessantly as it approached the signals displaying 'on', the driver doing his best to persuade the signalman to clear the road and so give him the chance of a good run at Sway bank. (Both JK)

Three different trains in the same direction. Far left is a borrowed Eastern Region V2 class 2-6-2 No. 60893 on the prestige down 'Bournemouth Belle' with the benefit of a clear road ahead. The V2 was one of six on loan to the Southern Region to cover a temporary shortfall in Southern Region motive power following the failure of No. 35020 at Crewkerne with a flawed driving axle in 1953. The V2s soon returned northwards. Comparing this image with that alongside and aprt from the different headcode and train, the lineside huts are different. Although as previously referred to as definitely of the permanent way variety, it is possible from the look of the original that this also doubled as a fog-mans hut, the duty of which was to place a detonator on the running rail when the distant signal was 'on' in times of poor visibility. Fog on the railway was defined in a particular way, each signal box having a predetermined fogging point and meaning a particular fixed object, which, if lost to the eye due to fog, which be the governing factor in calling out a fog man. Such staff were also members of the permanent way gang, hence the probable dual use for the hut. The trains seen are, a Brighton - Bournemouth working behind No. 34048 'Crediton' and T9 No. 30700 with a unknown service. (All JK)

Left - Another variant of motive power on the Brighton - Bournemouth services was the use of the BR 4MT tank engines. The Southern had often used large tank engines for a number of semi-fast workings so the appearance of a Brighton built example was no real surprise. Again the location is No. 7 Gates. (JK)

Right, top - 'Modern Image near Brockenhurst'. For a while during the early 1950s the total BR fleet of five diesel-electric locomotives, the LMS 'twins' Nos. 10000/1 and the SR trio 10201-3, were centred on the region with the intention of gaining operational experience of running a fleet of modern diesels. As such they were regular performers on both the Bournemouth and SR West of England lines, although, it must be said, not quite with the reliability that is expected of diesel traction nowadays. Partly this was due to unfamiliarity with the type, but it has also always appeared strange that the SR with its existing fleet of 140 Bulleid locomotives, plus all the Maunsell design 4-6-0s, should need five extra locomotives to cover similar roles. Whatever, on one of the days it was running, No. 10201 of 1750 hp rating heads east towards Southampton and Waterloo. (JK)

Right, bottom –Following the departure of the diesels to the London midland Region by 1955, the Southern Region in Hampshire reverted to being an almost exclusive steam railway, save that is for the existing electrified Portsmouth Direct, Alton - Farnham, and Portsmouth towards Chichester. Certainly it was not until 1957 that the growl of a diesel locomotive would be heard again on the main line, this time in the form of a test run with a new 'Hastings' unit, No. 1003 on a proving run from Waterloo to Bournemouth West, via Ringwood. Unfortunately the day did not go quite as had been planned for a motor bearing ran hot and the trial was terminated at Bournemouth. It was to be a temporary setback, the sets soon entering service on the Hastings line from Charing Cross, while later, technically similar diesel-electric two and three car trains commenced work on the Hampshire branch lines from Southampton. (JK)

Next page - Just west of Lyndhurst Road, a summer Saturday working labours east with some 18 coaches behind No. 75075. But all is not quite what it seems as this is in fact two trains - one in each direction, that seen approaching including a Western Region Collett design third as the first vehicle. The London bound service is hauled by a Bulleid Pacific. (JK)

Previous page - A final view of No. 7 gate crossing, a sparkling clean No. 70009 'Alfred the Great' on what is likely to be the down 'Bournemouth Belle'. The driver is seen looking backwards, possibly to see if the signalman has managed to clear the distant signal for a non-stop run through Brockenhurst - perhaps there was congestion at Lymington Junction, a conflicting movement in the station, the level crossing blocked with road traffic, or simply a train ahead. (JK)

Above - We now move east to Southampton Central and with it the commencement of the work of photographer Henry Meyer. Living in Winchester, Henry's visit on the Southern were restricted to a limited radius, although his imagery recorded the scene with great attention to detail and composition. According to the notes accompanying this view, he reported that T9s seemed to appear on almost every sort of train - possibly the generalisation should be 4-4-0s, as there were several similar types. Whatever, this is a genuine T9, No. 338, photographed in 1948 with a Cardiff to Portsmouth train of WR stock. Some platform repairs are evidently taking place on the left. (HM)

Right - Young train spotters admire No. 864 'Sir Martin Frobisher' at Southampton Central on the same day. Henry recalled that despite the number of youths present, there was never any problems between the enthusiasts and the station staff. (HM)

Left - The 'Bournemouth Belle' behind No. 34064 'Fighter Command'. This was usually a 'Merchant Navy' duty so the smaller locomotive may well have been a last minute replacement. The location is Northam, with the main line curve in the background and the connection to Southampton terminus via Tunnel Junction under the third coach to the right. Henry summed up us this view well, "Luxury travel passing great post-war deprivation in a corner of Southampton that somehow (just) managed to survive the blitz." He continued, "It was very difficult to get roll-film after the war, although some chemists did manage to get ex RAF film which they would cut into lengths of 120 size. It was very grainy, to an unknown speed and did not always wind on properly. Despite this it could be bought at a chemist near to where the photograph was taken". (HM)

Right - In the opposite direction No. 30746 'Pendragon' passes some unusual slate-hung houses at Six Dials, Southampton in 1950. Here outside toilets were the norm, as was having any washing hung outside specked with soot. (HM)

Above - Stoneham Sidings on the west side of the line south of Eastleigh, here four sidings were added in WW2, they survived intact until 1967. (In 2011 there is talk of reinstating at least one as a lay-by for container trains.) The Lord Nelson class engine is heading south towards Swaythling and displays a Bournemouth line headcode. Behind the photographer was the little Stoneham Signal Box which also controlled access over a local occupation crossing. The runway of Southampton Airport is across the field on the right. (HM)

Opposite - Eastleigh shed and its environs, 1949-56. Q1 No. 33005 seen reversing into the shed arrival roads. On the extreme right is the emergency crossover, rarely if ever used, but provided in case of blockage at the normal shed exit on to the main line. The 700 class engine will have taken the same route as the Q1 but stands at the coaling stage and disposal roads being serviced before being stabled ready for its next working. At the rear of the shed in 1956 is the restored LSWR T3 No. 563 waiting movement to Southampton Docks and road transport to preservation. Lurking within the shed it is just possible to make out the front end of another Lord Nelson the subject of inside cylinder valve examination. (All HM)

Above - North of Eastleigh and once past the end of the East Yard the railway ran for some distance on embankment above the water meadows and flood plain of the River Itchen. Henry Meyer recounted that on this particular photographic outing he was accompanied by two friends and that between taking photographs they diverted away to the river to swim and tickle trout. "We managed to tickle them but never caught one." In the meanwhile a London bound service passes in the background. **Right -** 15 June 1950: "The appearance of this locomotive (No. 36001) always caused great excitement. We really thought it would prolong the life of steam because whenever we saw it the performance seemed effortless." ('Leader' is heading north to Woking and eventually Guildford with a test train. This particular trial of 230 tons ended in failure.) (Both HM)

Opposite top - Still in SR livery, No. 21C161 '73 Squadron' heads north past Otterbourne intermediate block signals. 1948/9. (HM)

Opposite bottom - No. 741 'Joyous Guard' fitted with large chimney working an Up boat train. Henry's comment, "They were mostly dirty engines in those years although boat-train engines always seemed to be much cleaner than the rest." 1948/9. (HM)

Above - A rare glimpse of the access into the private siding at Otterbourne, courtesy of this 1951 view of No. 35017 'Belgian Marine'. The siding was accessed off the up local line and received coal, usually twice weekly, for the boilers at the water pumping station. (HM)

Above - "The sight of No. 629 approaching caused as excitement as the 'Leader'.....a rare and wonderful sight." This relic from an earlier age was recorded just south of Shawford station heading towards Eastleigh with a short engineers train. Years before the engine had been considered redundant and withdrawn in January 1939. It was reinstated in September 1939 and survived until December 1948.(HM)

Opposite page - Two views north of Shawford - between the station and Shawford Junction. 'Light Pacifics' are seen heading south in Southern and BR livery, respectively recorded in 1949 and 1950. In the background to the lower view the train is about to pass over the bridge carrying the infamous Winchester by-pass, itself now consigned to history. The chalk scar shows the course of the road at Hockley is visible in the background. Above this chalk the clump of trees stands at the top of St Catherine's Hill. If seen from the same location today an even greater scar of chalk signifies the route of the M3 motorway. (Both HM)

No. 21C11 north of Shawford with, it is believed, a Waterloo bound boat-train. 1948. (HM)

A wonderful collection of mixed vehicles although it is not possible to confirm if this was, as first appears, empty stock. Reverting back to Henry's earlier comment on cleanliness and he notes, "...these always seemed to be the dirtiest of them all…...and could not pull the skin off a rice pudding…." - referring to U class No. 31802 - BR number and ownership details. The train is on the Up main line immediately north of Shawford station and seems to be proceeding reasonably well. (HM)

This page, left - From the vantage point of the down relief line, No. 35014 'Nederland Line' heads up the 1-250 climb towards Shawford Junction. (HM)

This page, right - Shawford Junction, here the line to Newbury diverged, a N15X heading south with what is probably a Portsmouth working. 1950. (HM)

Opposite left and right - With Shawford Junction now behind us, the next station will be Winchester although first there is the short St Cross tunnel and level crossing / signal box of the same name. In the left image, the unidentified Lord Nelson heads north towards the tunnel, whilst on the right a King Arthur class engine is running in the opposite direction. 1950/1. (Both HM)

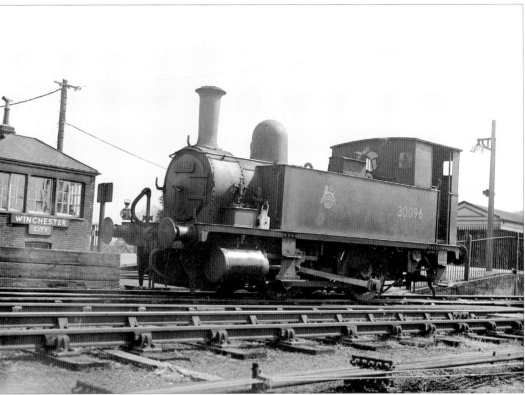

This page - Members of the B4 class acting as shunter / pilot at Winchester City. On the left No. 30089 has a rudimentary spark arrestor fitted - in appearance almost more like a metal hair-net - as it collects vans left in the down platform by a departed train. On the right, the more familiar and regular incumbent, No. 30096 stands opposite the old signal box in the area which forms part of the expansive station car-park. Together with sister engine No. 30102, these were the last members of the class to be employed at the station. Steam ceased to be used for shunting at Winchester City in October 1963, the B4 class reportedly having been used here since 1908. Post 1963 work was in the hands of a small diesel which remained as the regular shunter until the yard closed. (Left JK right HM)

Opposite page, left - The 'Bournemouth Belle' with its more usual Merchant Navy at the head - No. 35012 'United States Line' - comfortably running down the bank north of Winchester in 1950. (HM)

Opposite page, right - Firing time on M7 No. 30029 as it propels its push-pull train north towards Winchester Junction bound for Alton. 1950. (HM)

Above - M7 at speed. No. 109 working well as it propels its two coach Alton train along the main line past Abbotts Worthy on the way to Winchester Junction. Henry comments, "Drivers and firemen of local trains got to know the regular enthusiasts and always whistled a greeting - not so the express crews". (HM)
Opposite - The literal high point of the Bournemouth line: crossing over the west of England route at Battledown, believed to be No. 30754 'The Green Knight'. 1958. (HM)

We now move to the third contributor, Edward Griffiths. Edward was a professional photographer from Farnham and whilst recording the everyday scene for the local newspaper he was also very much a railway enthusiast for many years also a member of the REC. The views seen were supplied by Martin Upward although are unfortunately with caption details.

Opposite - Milk from the south west. (ECG)

Above - No. 30785 'Sir Mador de la Porta' - Maunsell locomotive and Bullied stock in Winchfield cutting. (ECG)

Externally, in almost as-built condition, save for the livery at least! No. 35013 'Blue Funnel' with original cab hauling the short lived Devon Belle Pullman service in Winchfield cutting. (ECG)

Top - Special workings and unusual locomotives for the July 1950 Farnborough air show. A number of special trains were run to this event, some of these originating on the former Great Eastern lines using air-brake stock. To cater for this on the Southern Region, former LBSCR locomotives equipped with Westinghouse air-pumps were brought in. Two examples, H1 No. 32421 'South Foreland' and a K class mogul are seen. The former engine is attached to a rake of GE stock. Notice the window-bars on the coach. (ECG)

Bottom - Main line working. The more usual scene, this time slightly further west at Fleet. A King Arthur heads west underneath the pneumatic gantry: the air reservoirs for the latter are seen at the base of the respective signal posts. (ECG)

Left - A Waterloo to Southampton Terminus local service waiting to leave Farnborough behind N15X No. 32327 'Trevithick'. (ECG)

Right - Main line workings, top to the west of England and bottom destined for the Bournemouth line. In both cases the location is Fleet and judging by the position of the open wagons in the siding, recorded shortly after each other. (Both ECG)

Overleaf - A chance, but fortunate encounter in Winchfield cutting. (ECG)